ANIMAL HIDEAWAYS

Written by
Anita Ganeri

Illustrated by
Halli Verrinder

Key Porter kids is an imprint of
Key Porter Books Limited
70 The Esplanade
Toronto, Ontario
Canada M5E 1R2

A Marshall Edition
Conceived, edited, and designed by Marshall Editions
170 Piccadilly, London, England W1V 9DD

Copyright © 1996 by Marshall Editions Developments Ltd.

Editor: Jolika Feszt
Designer: Sandra Begnor
Consultant: Dr. Philip Whitfield
Editorial director: Cynthia O'Brien
Art director: Branka Surla

Canadian Cataloguing in Publication Data

Ganeri, Anita, 1961–
Animal hideaways

ISBN 1-55013--715-8

1. Animal – Habitations – Juvenile literature.
2. Toy and movable books.
I. Title

QL756.G35 1995   j591.56'4   C95-932022-9

World Wildlife Fund works to save wildlife and wild places in
Canada and around the world. To find out how you can help, call 1–800–26–PANDA.

Printed in Italy
by Editoriale Libraria

96 97 98 99 5 4 3 2 1

Contents

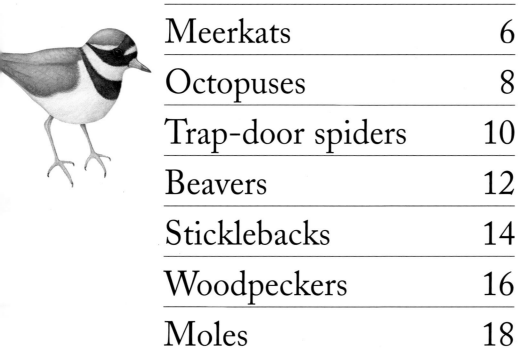
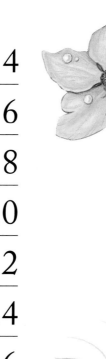

Plovers	4
Meerkats	6
Octopuses	8
Trap-door spiders	10
Beavers	12
Sticklebacks	14
Woodpeckers	16
Moles	18
Honeybees	20
Polar bears	22
Index	24

Plovers

The ringed plover lives by the sea on sandy or pebbly beaches. The female does not build a nest. Instead she lays her eggs among the pebbles where the eggs' spotted shells hide them from hungry gulls. The mother's coloring also makes her difficult to see.

Plovers have long legs for wading through the shallows in search of food. They eat shellfish, insects, and worms.

4

If an enemy comes too close, the mother plover pretends to be injured to lead it away from her eggs. Then she flies off.

The plover usually lays four eggs. After they hatch, both parents care for the young.

5

Meerkats

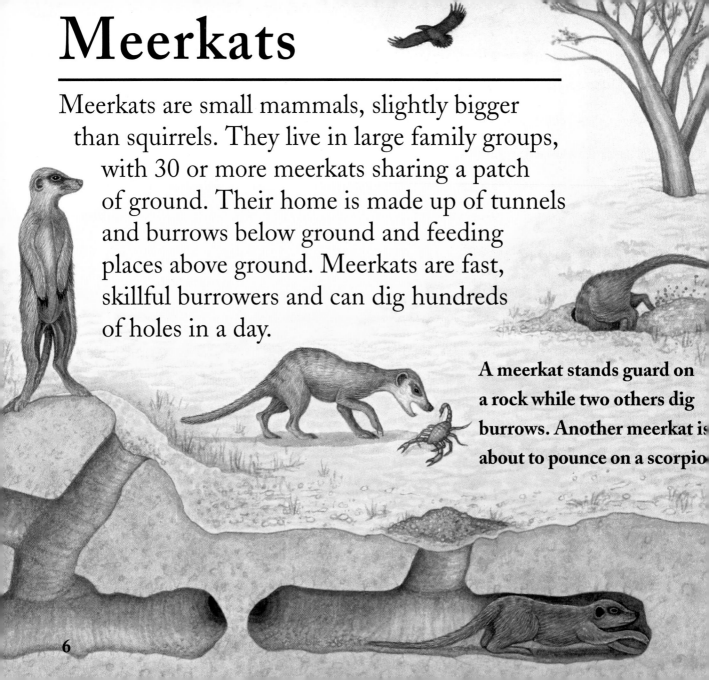

Meerkats are small mammals, slightly bigger than squirrels. They live in large family groups, with 30 or more meerkats sharing a patch of ground. Their home is made up of tunnels and burrows below ground and feeding places above ground. Meerkats are fast, skillful burrowers and can dig hundreds of holes in a day.

A meerkat stands guard on a rock while two others dig burrows. Another meerkat is about to pounce on a scorpio

6

At the first sign of danger, the guard sounds
the alarm and the meerkats dive into their
burrows. Their main enemies are birds
of prey, jackals, and foxes.

7

Octopuses

Octopuses hunt for food at night. By day they hide away in their dens in a coral reef. A den is hard to spot, with a tiny crack just big enough for an octopus to squeeze through. The female lays her eggs in the den, guarding them day and night until they hatch.

An octopus eats crabs. It creeps up on its prey, grabs the crab in a long tentacle, and kills it with a poisonous bite.

Crab

The octopus shown here is called Octopus briareus. It lives off the east coast of Florida.

9

Trap-door spiders

The trap-door spider digs an underground burrow with a lid or trapdoor across the top. Holding the trapdoor shut with its fangs, it waits until a bug runs past. Then it rushes out, grabs the insect, and drags it into its burrow. Trap-door spiders use their fangs as shovels for digging burrows. The walls of the burrow are coated with soil and a kind of spit to make them waterproof.

Trap-door spiders eat insects such as bugs, beetles, and millipedes, as well as other spiders.

The trap-door spider sits inside the burrow.

It waits for suitable prey to arrive.

Then it quickly springs out to capture its prey.

Most trap-door spiders live in warm places. This spider is from California.

The burrow is about eight inches deep.

11

Beavers

Beavers live in homes of wood and mud called lodges. A beaver family constructs a dam of sticks, stones, and mud across a river or stream to form a deep pond. The beavers then build a lodge where they are safe from wolves and other enemies.

Beavers often store some logs underwater. In winter when the pond freezes over, these logs are used for repairs and the bark provides food.

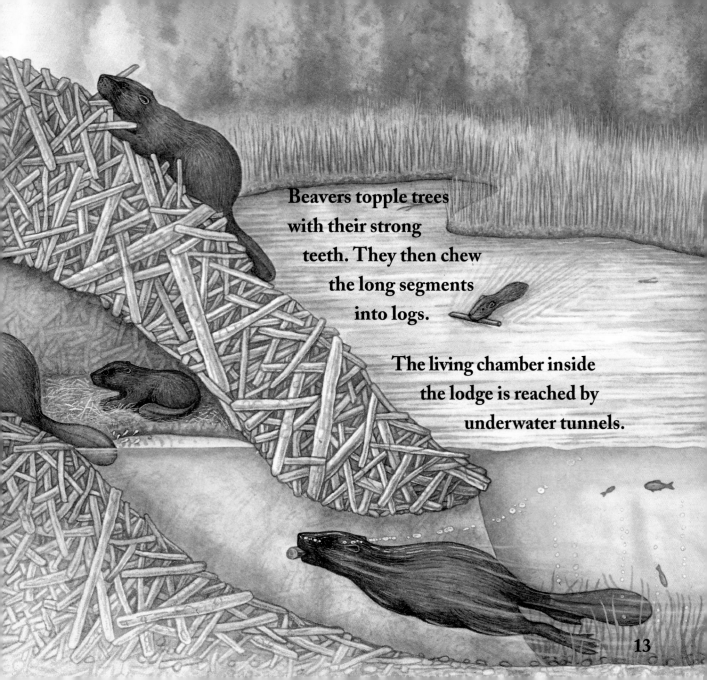

Beavers topple trees
with their strong
teeth. They then chew
the long segments
into logs.

The living chamber inside
the lodge is reached by
underwater tunnels.

13

Sticklebacks

The three-spined stickleback is an unusual fish because it builds a nest, just like a bird. The male stickleback makes the nest in spring. When it is finished, he dances around it to attract a female. She inspects the nest and lays her eggs inside it. After a week, the eggs hatch. For the first few days, the baby fish stay close to their father.

The male builds his nest on the sandy bed of a river or stream. He clears the spot, then digs a shallow pit with his mouth.

At breeding time, the male stickleback's throat and belly turn bright red. This helps him attract a mate.

14

The male stickleback makes a tunnel-shaped nest from waterweeds. Here, the female lays her eggs, as shown below.

Woodpeckers

A loud *tap, tap, tapping* sound in a forest may be a woodpecker pecking out a hole in a tree trunk with its sharp, strong beak. The hole is used as a nest for raising young birds. The female woodpecker lays three to five glossy white eggs in the nest. Then both parents take turns looking after them until the eggs hatch. The bird shown here is called a pileated woodpecker.

Woodpeckers love to eat ants, worms, grubs, spiders, and berries.

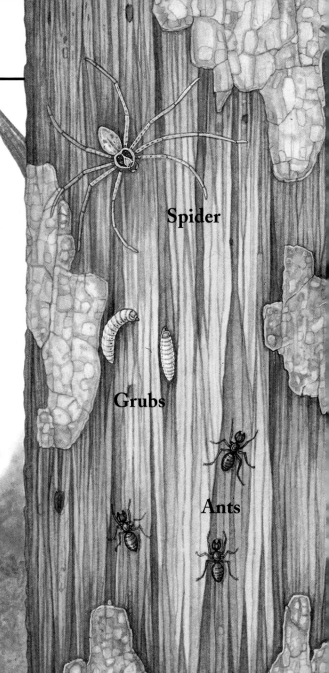

Spider

Grubs

Ants

The eggs take three weeks to hatch. Little chicks are always hungry! Their parents are kept busy bringing them food.

Pileated woodpeckers live in the forests and woods of Canada and the United States.

17

Moles

Most of a mole's home lies underground. Piles of soil are pushed up to the surface as the mole digs a network of tunnels and burrows below. Because moles spend most of their lives hidden underground, they cannot see very well. They rely on their senses of touch and smell instead.

The piles of soil on the surface are called molehi

Moles feed on earthworms that they dig out of the soil.

18

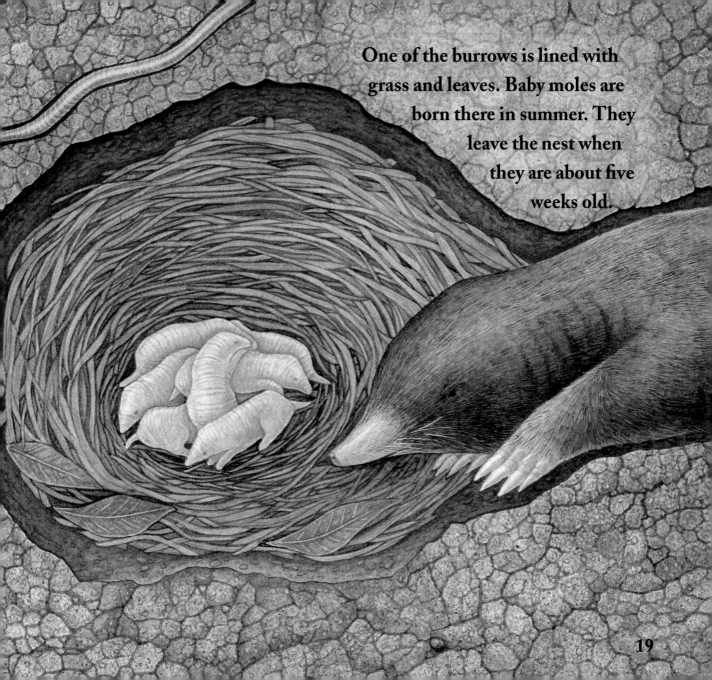

One of the burrows is lined with grass and leaves. Baby moles are born there in summer. They leave the nest when they are about five weeks old.

Honeybees

Honeybees are very sociable. Thousands of them may live together in a nest, which they often build inside hollow tree trunks. Here, bees make a honeycomb of six-sided chambers, called cells. Some cells are used to store honey. Others are used as nurseries for eggs and baby bees, called grubs.

The honeyguide bird from Africa eats bee grubs and beeswax. The bird gets its name from the way it guides people and other mammals to bees' nests.

Honeyguide

Most of the bees are worker bees. They build the cells, keep them clean, and look after the grubs.

The cells inside the honeycomb are made of wax from the bees' bodies. The bees mix the wax with spit until it is soft enough to mold into shape.

The worker bees collect flower pollen and nectar to make into honey. Some of the honey is stored in the nest for when food is hard to find.

Polar bears

In winter it is freezing cold and icy in the Arctic where polar bears live. But polar bear cubs stay snug and warm in their den beneath the snow. In the spring they venture outside with their mother to explore and hunt for food.

The mother bear digs her den in autumn. She uses her huge paws as snow shovels.

Air hole

A polar bear's favorite food is seal. The bear waits patiently by a hole in the ice until a seal comes up for air from the water below.

23

Index

A
Africa 20
ants 16
Arctic 22

B
beavers 12–13
beetles 10
berries 16
birds of prey 7
bugs 10
burrows 6–7, 10–11, 18–19

C
California 11
Canada 17
crabs 8

D
dens 8, 22

E
eggs 4–5, 8, 14, 16–17, 20

F
Florida 9
foxes 7

G
grubs 16, 20

H
honey 20, 21
honeybees 20–21
honeyguide bird 20

I
insects 4, 10

J
jackals 7

L
lodges 12–13

M
meerkats 6–7
millipedes 10
molehills 18
moles 18–19

N
nests 4, 14–15, 16, 20–21

O
octopus briareus 8–9

P
plover, ringed 4–5
polar bears 22–23

S
scorpions 6
seals 23
shellfish 4
spiders 10, 16
   trap-door 10–11
stickleback, three-spined 14–15

T
tunnels 6, 13, 18

U
United States 17

W
wolves 12
woodpecker, pileated 16–17
worms 4, 16, 18